MW00443377

Dedication
This book is dedicated to the generous and talented photographers who made their images available to us for this book. Thank you.

Have a question or concern? Let us know.
FritzenPublishing.com | support@fritzenpublishing.com

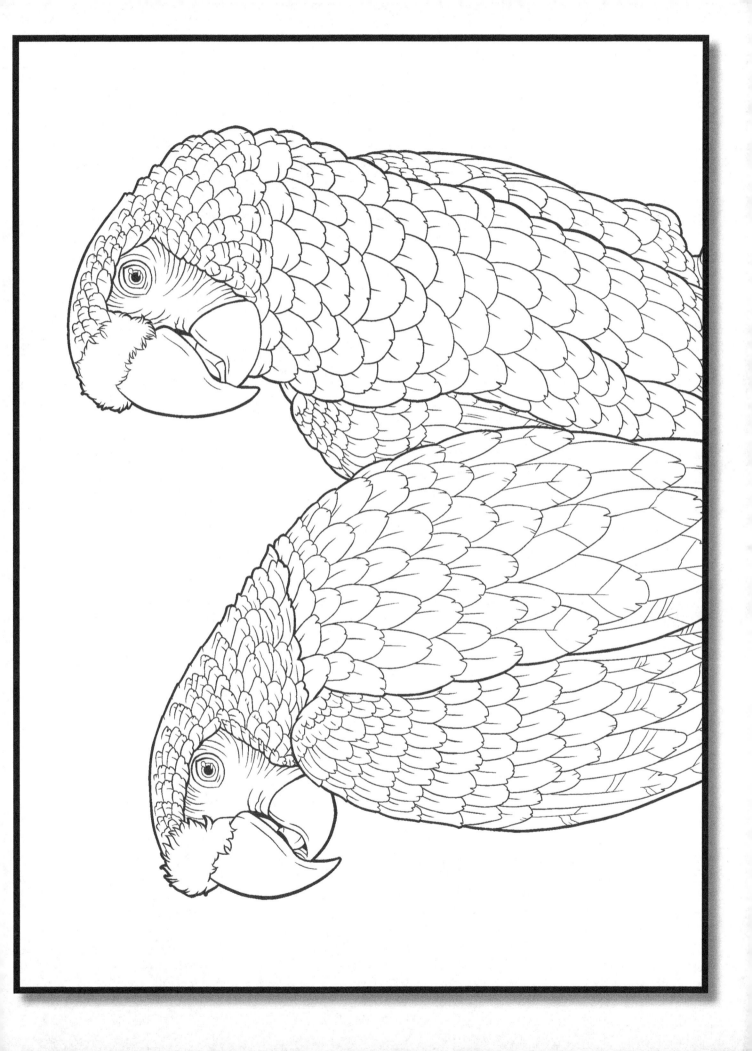

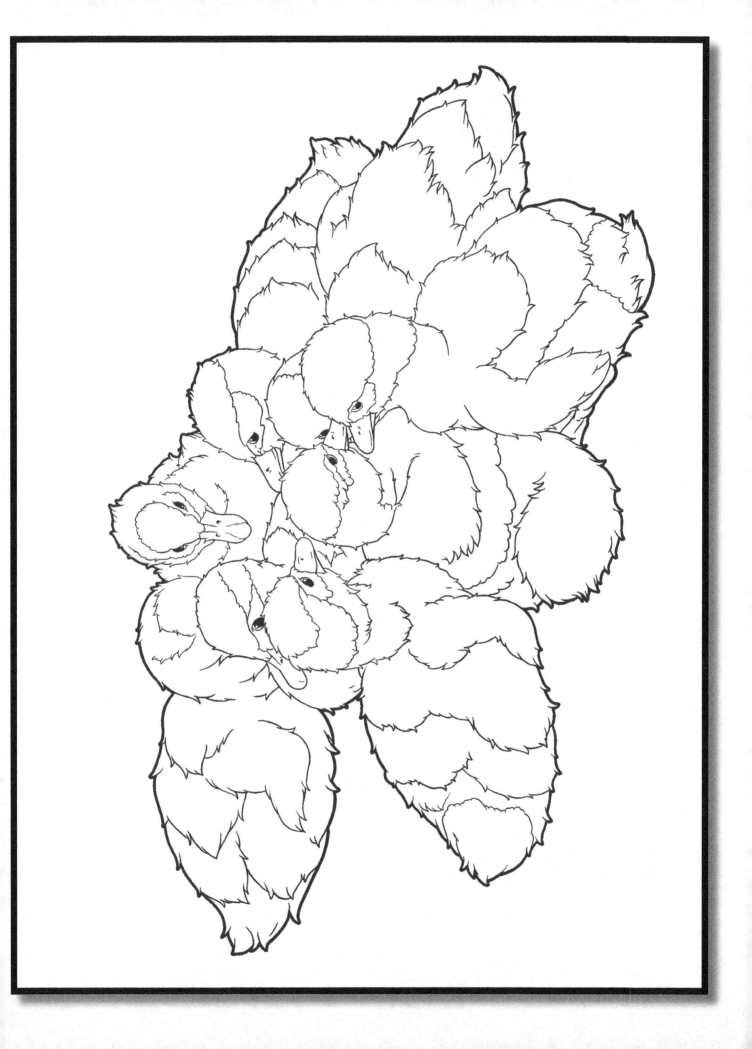

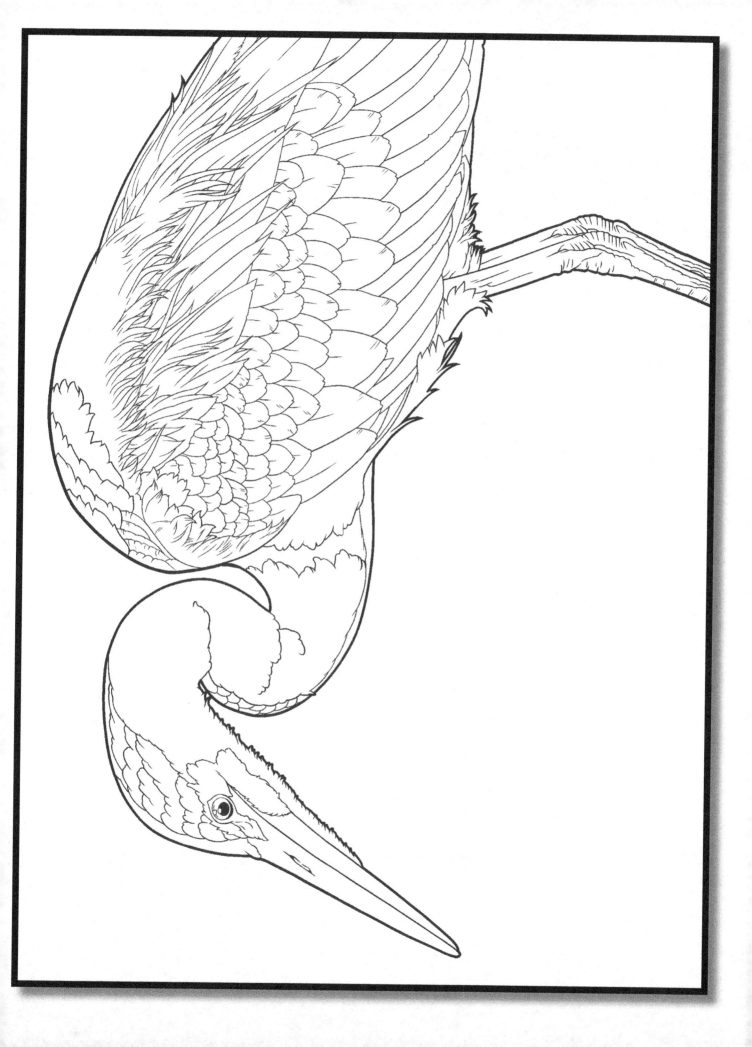

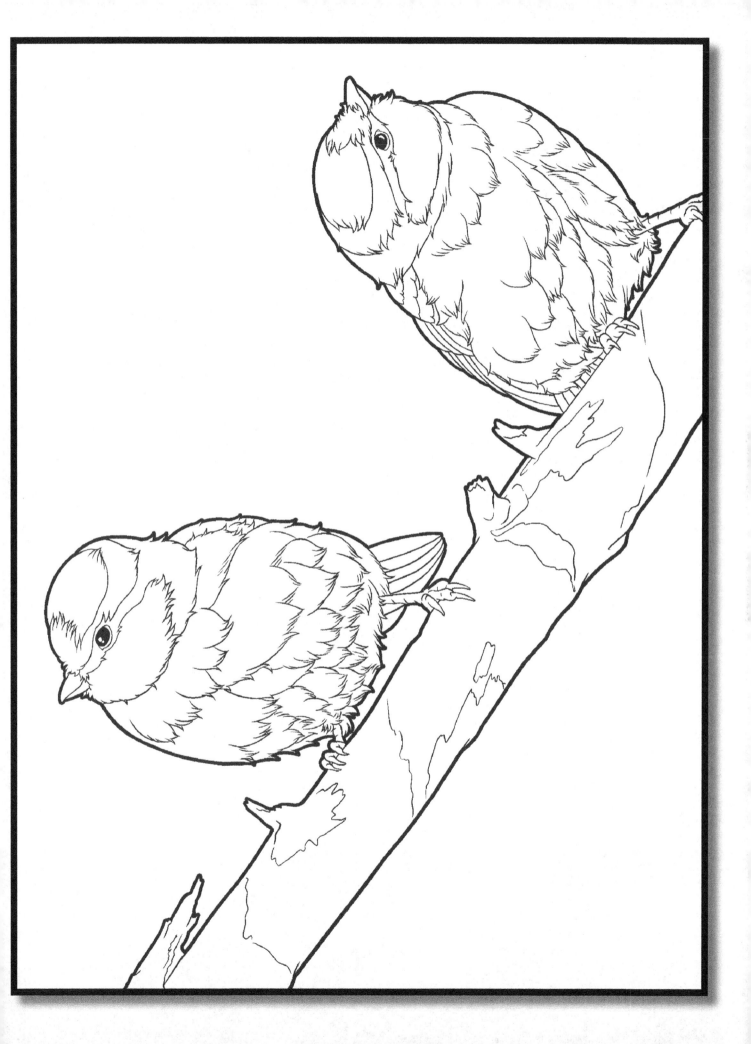

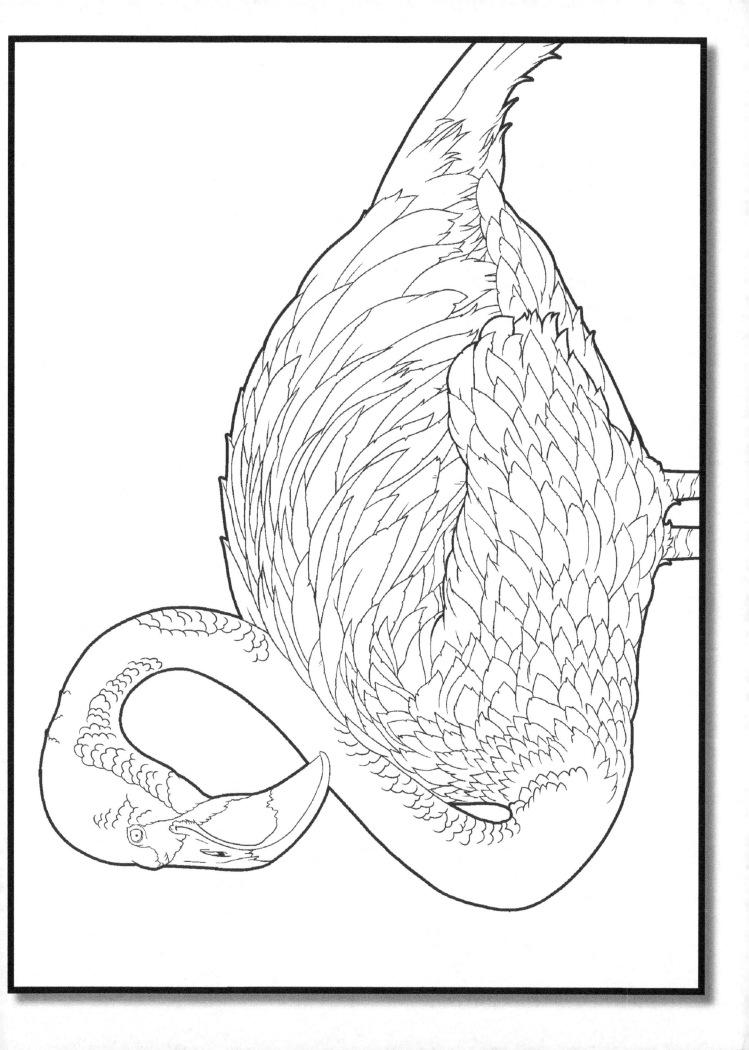

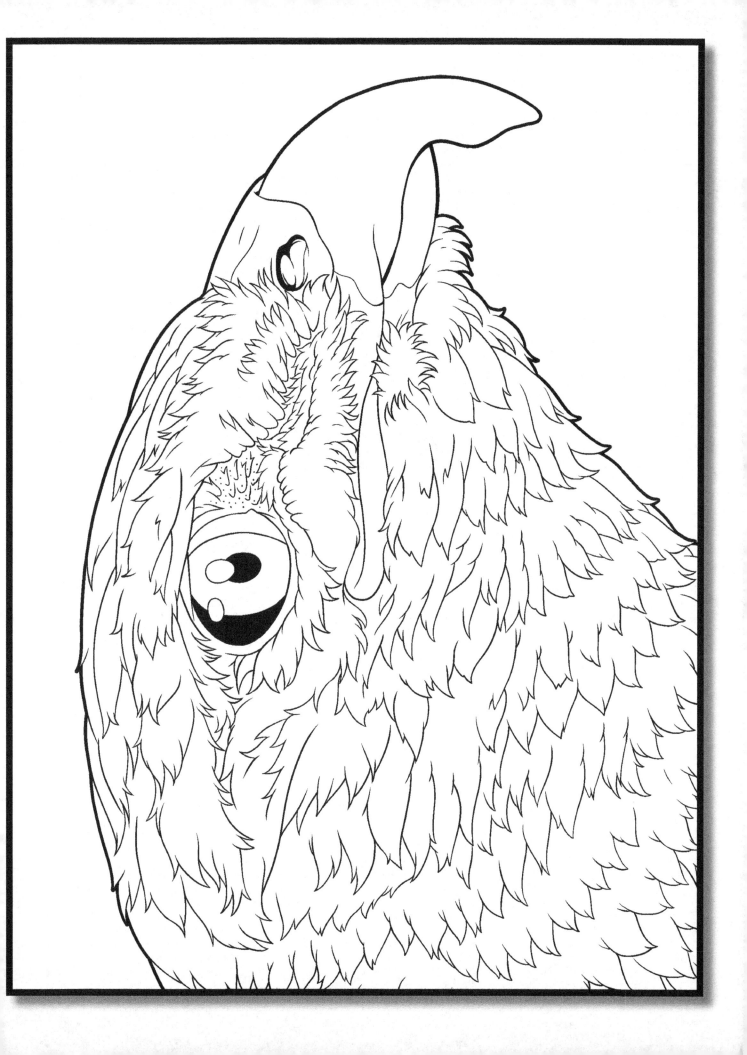

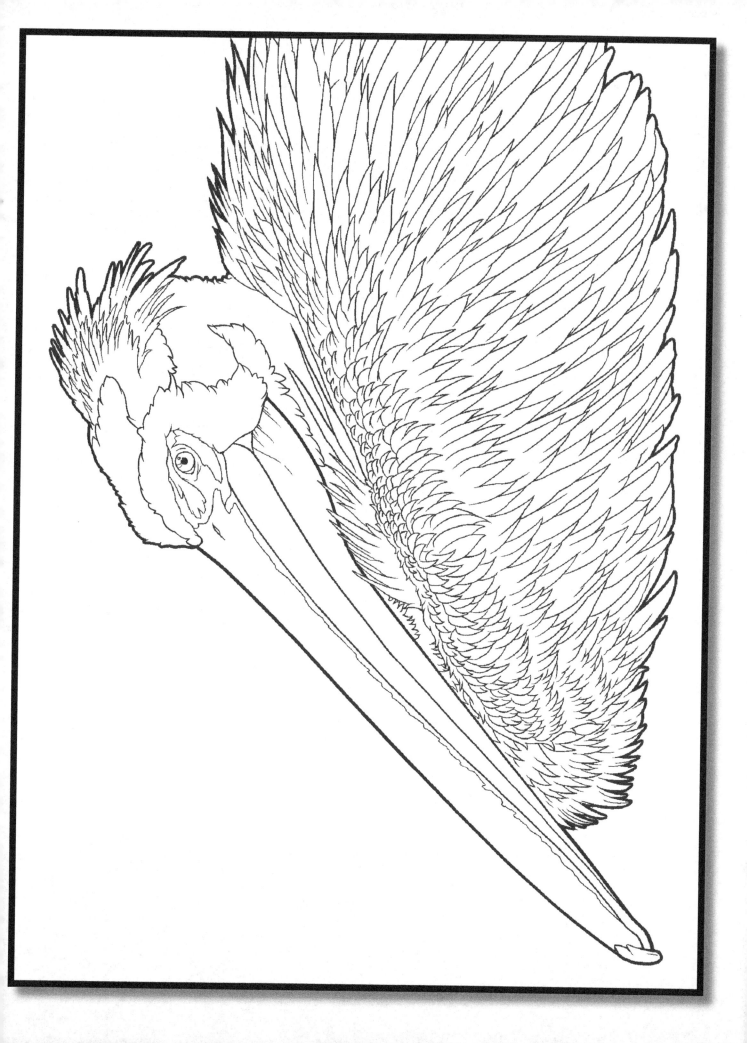

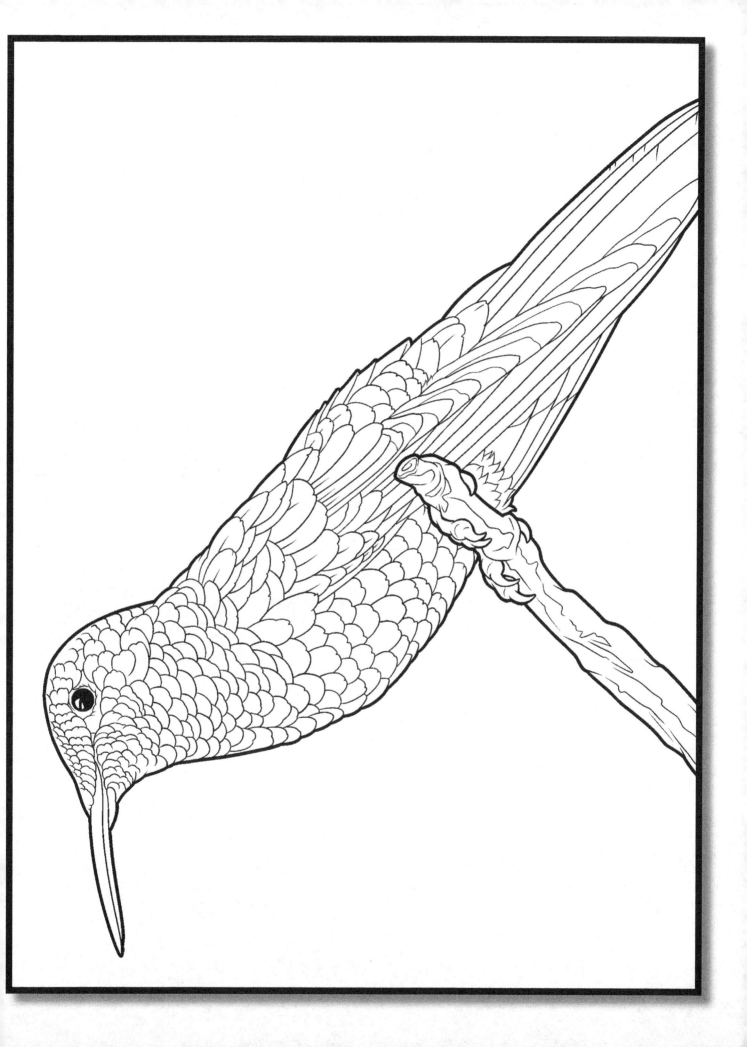

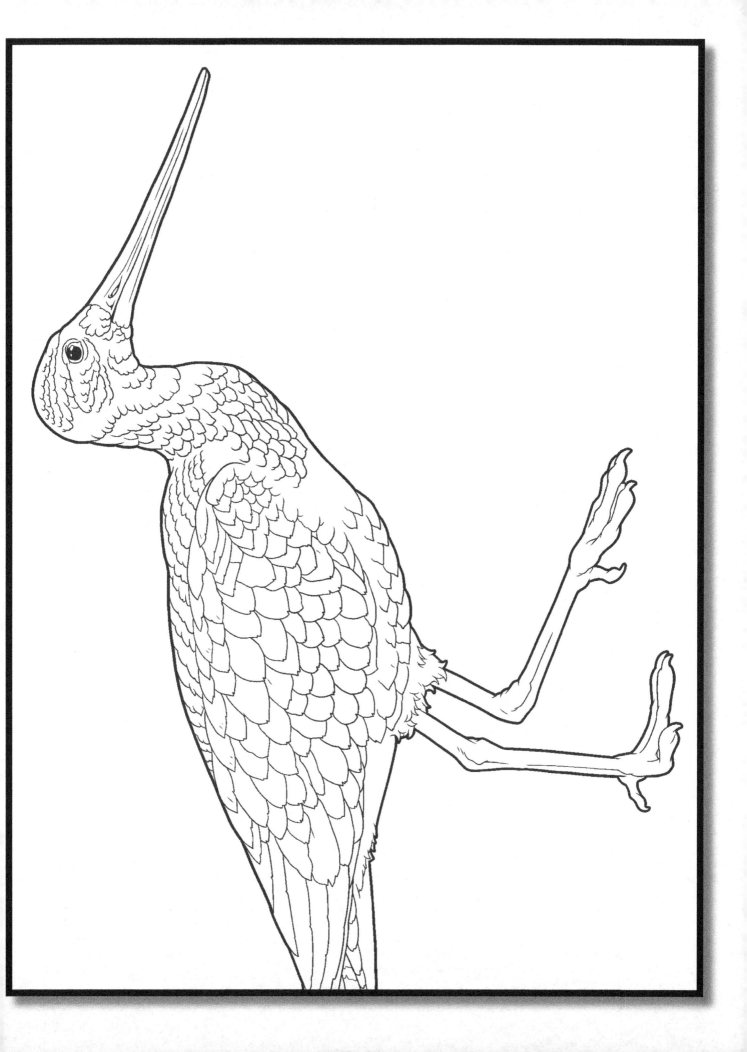

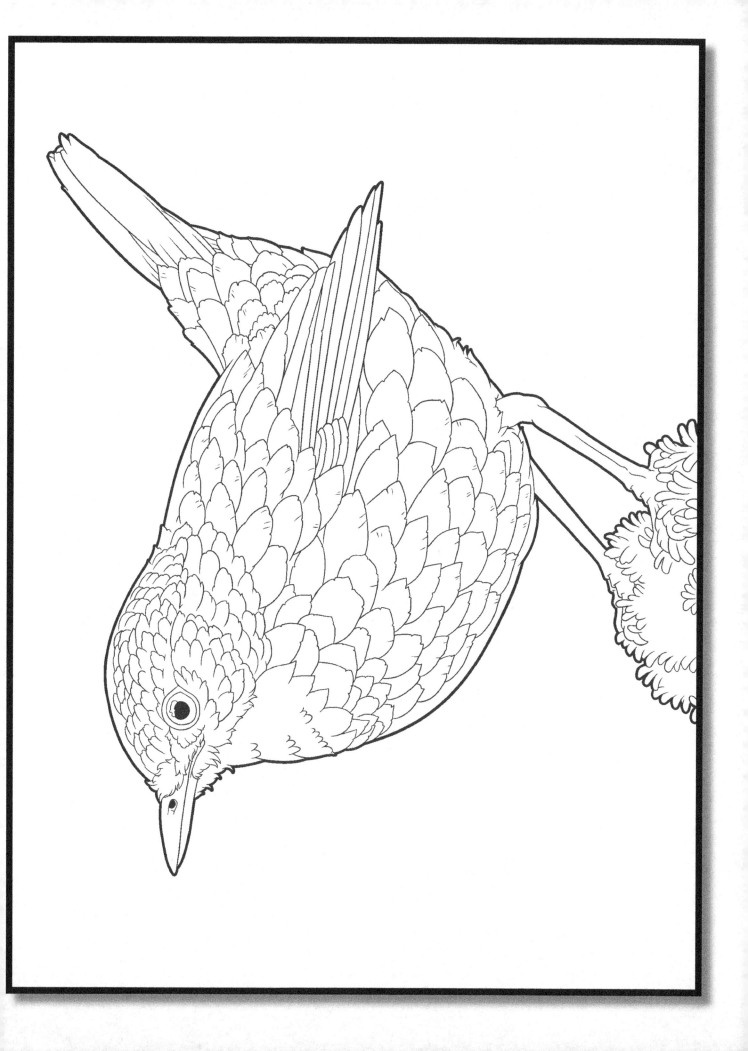

LEAVE YOUR AMAZON REVIEW

Show your support for Jade Summer and help other colorists discover our artwork.

Amazon reviews are essential for our business.

Simply find this book on Amazon, scroll to the customer reviews, and share your thoughts.

We appreciate your reviews very much. Thank you.

JOIN OUR EMAIL LIST

Join now on JadeSummer.com.
We will email you when new books are available.
Don't miss out on new release sales and other deals.

JOIN OUR ARTWORK GROUP

Search for *Jade Summer Artwork* on Facebook.
View completed pages from fans, share your thoughts, and discover more about Jade Summer.

FIND YOUR NEXT BOOK ON JADESUMMER.COM

Make your wish list or gift list. Know someone who loves to color?

- __ Alice in Wonderland
- __ Alice's Adventures...
- __ Amazing Animals
- __ Ancient Egypt
- __ Angels
- __ Animal Mandalas
- __ Animal Mandalas (2018)
- __ Animals for Beginners
- __ Animals Grayscale
- __ Anime Coloring Book
- __ Awesome Animals #1
- __ Awesome Animals #2
- __ Baby Dragons
- __ Be F*cking Awesome...
- __ Beautiful Birds
- __ Beautiful Butterflies
- __ Beautiful Dresses
- __ Beautiful Flowers
- __ Calm the F*ck Down...
- __ Chibi Animals
- __ Chibi Girls #1
- __ Chibi Girls #2
- __ Chibi Girls Grayscale
- __ Chibi Girls Horror
- __ Chill the F*ck Out...
- __ Christmas #1
- __ Christmas #2
- __ Christmas Animals
- __ Christmas Flowers
- __ Christmas for Kids
- __ Christmas for Toddlers
- __ Christmas Mandalas
- __ Color Charts
- __ Costume Cats
- __ Country Farm
- __ Cute Animals
- __ Cute Cats
- __ Cute Fairies
- __ Cute Unicorns

- __ Cute Witches
- __ Dark Fantasy
- __ Delicious Desserts
- __ Delicious Food
- __ Dinosaurs for Kids
- __ Dragons
- ✓ Easter
- __ Edgar Allan Poe
- __ Elegant Elephants
- __ Emoji
- __ Everyday Horror
- __ Fairies
- __ Fantasy Adventure
- __ Fantasy Collection #1
- __ Fantasy Grayscale
- __ Favorite Pages
- __ Flower Girls
- __ Flower Mandalas
- __ Flowers for Beginners
- __ Flowers Grayscale
- __ Greatest Hits
- __ Greek Mythology
- __ Grimm Fairy Tales
- __ Haunted House
- __ Henna
- __ Hidden Garden
- __ Horses
- __ Inspirational Quotes
- __ Inspirational Words
- __ Island Paradise
- __ Kawaii Girls
- __ Kickass Cats
- __ Lazy Dogs
- __ Light Fantasy
- __ Little Red Riding Hood
- __ Live Your Dreams
- __ Magical Forest
- __ Magical Mandalas
- __ Magical Swirls

- __ Magnificent Mandalas
- __ Mandala Animals #1
- __ Mandala Animals #2
- __ Mandala Animals #3
- __ Mandalas for Beginners
- __ Mandalas for Kids
- __ Mermaids
- __ Mermaids (2018)
- __ Naughty Animals
- __ Norse Mythology
- __ Oceans
- __ Pride & Prejudice
- __ Princesses
- __ Proud to be a Girl
- __ Psalms
- __ Red Riding Hood
- __ Relaxing Animals
- __ Relaxing Designs
- __ Relaxing Flowers
- __ Secret Jungle
- __ Springtime Animals
- __ Springtime Flowers
- __ Stuffed Animals
- __ Sugar Skulls
- __ Tattoos
- __ Under the Sea
- __ Unicorns
- __ Vampires #1
- __ Vampires #2
- __ Vampires #1 & #2
- __ Vampires Grayscale
- __ Victorian Fashion
- __ What Women Want
- __ Wonderful Christmas

Made in the USA
Monee, IL
02 May 2020